Jim Carrey: Comic Ace

by Deborah Felder

A Bullseye Book

Random House New York

For Heather and Elizabeth Baker, with much love

Photo Credits: Larry Laszlo/CoMedia, p. 33; Photofest, pgs. 25–32; Vincent Zuffante/ Star File, p. 33; Richard Perry/Sygma, p. 34.

A BULLSEYE BOOK PUBLISHED BY RANDOM HOUSE, INC.
Copyright © 1995 by Deborah Felder
All rights reserved under International and Pan-American Copyright Conventions.
Published in the United States by Random House, Inc., New York, and simultaneously in Canada by Random House of Canada Limited, Toronto.

Library of Congress Cataloging-in-Publication Data:
Felder, Deborah G.
Jim Carrey : comic ace / by Deborah Felder.
   p.   cm.
"A Bullseye book."
ISBN 0-679-87448-8 (pbk.)
1. Carrey, Jim, 1962– . 2. Comedians—United States—Biography—Juvenile literature.   3. Motion picture actors and actresses—United States—Biography—Juvenile literature. [1. Carrey, Jim, 1962– . 2. Actors and actresses.
3. Comedians.] I. Title. PN2287.C278F46 1995
791.43'028'092—dc20
[B] 95-26
Manufactured in the United States of America 10 9 8 7 6 5 4 3 2 1

Contents

Chapter 1

Who Is This Mask Man?

"Alone at last," Jim Carrey said with a sigh. For the first time, Jim isn't being mobbed by reporters and photographers. Finally he can relax, as he settles into his airline seat.

It's spring 1994. Jim is on his way back to the U.S. from France, where he was the star attraction at the famous Cannes Film Festival. He went to the festival to promote his new movie, *The Mask*. That meant nonstop interviews and photo sessions. And, of course, there was a special screening of *The*

Mask. Everyone at the festival thought the movie would be a big hit.

They were wrong. When *The Mask* hit theaters all across America that summer, it wasn't just a big hit—it was a *mega*hit! Jim's role as mild-mannered nice-guy bank clerk Stanley Ipkiss, who puts on an ancient Viking mask and immediately morphs into s-s-snazzy wiseguy superhero The Mask, wowed audiences. And Jim became an even hotter movie star than he was before.

The year 1994 has been an awesome one for Jim Carrey. First he burst onto the movie scene in a major way with the surprise hit *Ace Ventura: Pet Detective*. Then he pulled out all the comic stops in *The Mask*. And on top of that, while he was in France, he found out that he had bagged the plum role of the Riddler in the newest Batman movie, *Batman Forever*.

But even on the plane back from Cannes, Jim is getting into a work mode. After his stay in France, he is headed out west. His next movie, *Dumb and Dumber,* is being filmed in Utah.

A limo takes him to the outskirts of a little town near the set of *Dumb and Dumber.* It's very different from the noisy, crowded scene at the Cannes Film Festival. Here, there are silent wide-open spaces with beautiful snowcapped mountains all around. And that's fine with Jim. Even a superstar who loves his fans and loves to make people laugh needs some quiet time.

Or does he?

While he's waiting for filming to begin, Jim goes into his trailer. He's wearing his *Dumb and Dumber* costume—goofy shoes, a plaid coat, and fringed gloves. His hair is plastered down and he's taken the cap off his chipped front tooth. When he was a kid, he chipped his tooth in an accident. He's showing it off to audiences for the first time in *Dumb and Dumber.*

Alone in the trailer, Jim listens to a Tom Petty CD. He turns up the volume to the max and starts rockin' to the music. Soon, the trailer is shaking, bouncing up and down on its tires to the beat of the music. Then Jim kicks open the door and stands in the doorway, yelling, "I love Tom Petty! Tom Petty's great!"

That's Jim Carrey—from quiet to riot in nanoseconds!

Chapter 2

Jimmy-Gene, the String Bean

Whenever Jim Carrey shows up, zaniness always seems to follow. Would you believe that he was once a shy, quiet kid who liked to draw pictures and write poetry? Or that his childhood nickname was Jimmy-Gene, the String Bean? Or that he left high school in tenth grade?

It's all true.

Jim was born James Eugene Carrey on January 17, 1962, in Newmarket, Ontario,

Canada. He spent his early childhood in the nearby small town of Aurora. Both Newmarket and Aurora are about thirty miles north of Toronto, Canada's largest city.

Jim was the youngest of four children of Percy and Kathleen Carrey. Even as a baby, Jim showed a talent for being funny. His sister, Pat, remembers him sitting in his high chair and making funny faces that would get laughs from everyone around him.

Besides being the comic kid, Jim had some other hobbies as well. He liked to draw—so much, he said, that "if my mother asked me to do something else, I'd have a hairy conniption. I'd just go crazy."

As a young boy, Jim spent most of his time on his own or with his family. He said he didn't have a single friend until third grade.

Jim also kept busy writing poetry. He can still recite some of the poems he wrote as a child.

But even though Jim was a shy kid, there was a natural-born riot underneath all that quiet. When he wasn't drawing or writing, he was looking for ways to make people laugh. He spent hours in front of the mirror making funny faces. He spent so much time twisting his face into strange shapes that his mother started to worry about him. Once, when he was trying out a really weird expression, she told him his face would freeze that way. She hoped it would scare him into leaving his face alone, in its natural position. It didn't.

When Jim was in third grade, his family moved to Toronto. "That was when I broke out of my shell at school," Jim said. "I did this zany thing and all of a sudden I had tons of friends." He had found his audience.

Chapter 3

A Class Act

As Jim got older, he worked hard at school. He was a good student who finished his work quickly. After completing his assignments, he would look around the classroom for a chance to make the other students laugh. His teacher finally said, "If you think you're so funny, Mr. Carrey, why don't you come up to the front of the class and try it from here?" So Jim did just that. On the spur of the moment, he made up a routine in which he pretended to be all of the Three Stooges. His classmates roared with laughter. The teacher wasn't impressed. But that didn't stop Jim! In fact, he took his comic genius home, too.

Jim was a one-kid comedy show. He'd entertain his family—and anyone else who showed up at the Carrey house—with his own special kind of slapstick. "Every time there was a new person in the house, it was time for the 'Jim Carrey Show,'" he said. One of his favorite tricks was to tumble down the stairs in real speed. Then he'd go back upstairs and do it again—this time in slow motion. "It became nuts," said Jim. "I started sleeping in my tap shoes in case my parents needed a laugh during the night." His parents couldn't take him to restaurants because, said Jim, "I'd go into my act."

Jim did impressions, too. He'd imitate his grandparents, neighbors, and famous TV stars. His favorite comedian was Jerry Lewis, who played ultra-goofy characters in movies of the 1950s and 1960s, like *The Nutty Professor*. Later, when Jim became a stand-up comic, he included a little Jerry Lewis–type humor in his act.

Then there were the famous Carrey family food fights. When Jim had friends over for dinner, "It was just a matter of time before somebody got half a pound of butter smeared across their face." Sundays in the Carrey household were special: "We'd have a cherry cheesecake fight!"

When Jim was in junior high school, one teacher gave him fifteen minutes to perform at the end of the school day. Jim would chew up a pack of heart-shaped powdered candies. Then he'd pretend he was sick and throw up all the different-colored candies. "For no reason," he said. "Just that I could do it." His classmates loved it. And Jim loved being class clown. "Acting goofy became my motivation for living," he said.

Jim was popular, and he was getting straight A's. But tough times were ahead for the Carrey family. When Jim was thirteen, his father was laid off from his job. Percy Carrey had been a saxophone player and band leader but had given up his work as a musician and band leader to become an accountant. When he lost his accountant's job, the family became, in Jim's words, "financially devastated." Jim's dad was fifty-one years old, and he couldn't find another job. To make ends meet, Jim, his parents, and two of his three siblings went to work at the Titan Wheels factory in Toronto. It was a factory that made steel tire rims. Jim worked there as a security guard and janitor.

At first, the Carreys lived in factory-owned housing. They moved out of there and into a Volkswagen van. "We lived all around Toronto," Jim said. "It wasn't a real happy time." For a while, Jim's family even lived in a tent pitched on his eldest sister's lawn. "We were gypsies," said Jim. "It was weird." Today, when people ask Jim about the pressures of being in show business, he said, "Nothing compares to the pressure of living in a van. Everything else is a step up." It took the Carreys nearly two years before they could move back into a house.

At school, the stress on Jim was beginning to show. Jim slept in class because he was working in the factory for eight hours after school. "I went from being the top student in the class to 'I don't understand a word you're saying,'" he said. "I was so angry, I didn't want to hear it. I didn't have any friends because I didn't want them." Jim's hard times have made him understand better how family problems can affect teens: "If it's bad at home, you ain't got an easy deal." Yet even through the difficult times, Jim said his family always stayed together. "We had problems like all families, but we had a lot of love. I was extremely loved. We always felt we had each other."

When Jim was in tenth grade, he made a very serious decision. He decided to drop out of school. He might have stayed at the Titan Wheels factory forever. Instead, he made another move that would change his life. He was about to take his first step up—onto the ladder of success. And he had already decided how he would climb that ladder—by making people laugh.

Little did Jim know that climbing one step at a time would only last for so long. For Jim Carrey, soaring to stardom was more his style!

Chapter 4

Funny and Funnier

Jim's parents had always encouraged their son's comic talent. When Jim was fifteen or sixteen, his father took him to Yuk Yuks, a hip Toronto comedy club, for his first performance as a stand-up comic. His mom made him wear a yellow polyester suit for the occasion. "This is what they wear," she told him. He also took a prop with him—a ventriloquist's dummy.

How did Jim's suit and stand-up act stand up at Yuk Yuks? Not too well. In fact, he was booed off the stage!

But Jim didn't give up. Two years later,

he went back to Yuk Yuks without the dummy, wearing different clothes, and with a new act. Jim's new comedy routine featured lots of loopy impressions of celebrities. "I messed my hair up," he said. "No polyester. It was great. Comedy had changed my life."

Jim worked at odd jobs during the day. At night, he drove 100 miles round-trip for his chance to be in the limelight at Yuk Yuks. At first his father went with him. But after a while, Jim wanted to be on his own. He told his dad he could do it alone and to go back home. He was going to be okay.

Jim's career began to take off. Soon he was making people laugh in comedy clubs all over Canada. And more important, his success also enabled him to help his family out financially.

One of Jim's first fans was the comedian

Rodney Dangerfield, who later hired Jim to be his opening act in Canada. "He was really sensational, an unusual talent," Dangerfield once said. "He could make his face into anything."

By the time Jim was nineteen, he was a major star in Canada. But he felt his Canadian career had gone about as far as it could go. He was getting offers to perform in the U.S., invitations to appear on *The Tonight Show*. He was ready for some big-time fame and fortune in the U.S.!

Chapter 5

A Comedy in Living Colors

Jim packed his bags and headed for Los Angeles to try his luck. He lived in cheap motel rooms while he was struggling to make it in L.A.'s comedy clubs. Soon, he was winning raves for his act and performing regularly at L.A.'s famed Comedy Store, where many top comedians have appeared. During his act, Jim would take requests from the audience. They would ask him to do impressions of famous people. Jim would then make up an instant routine about the celebrity. Audiences loved it!

Along the way, Jim met a comedy-club waitress named Melissa. They fell in love and got married. Soon after, they had a baby girl, whom they named Jane. Funnyman Jim was now a family man as well.

At work, Jim was earning standing ovations every night. He was making lots of money too. But his act just didn't feel right. It consisted only of "tributes to famous people, just very standard impressions," he said. "It was so limiting. I decided to start from scratch. Everybody told me I was nuts."

He quit the stand-up business for a while and spent some time painting and sculpting. He also took acting lessons. In 1984, he moved another step up the ladder when he won the starring role in an NBC sitcom, *The Duck Factory*.

In the show, Jim played a cartoonist at a

small, run-down Hollywood animation studio working on a cartoon show called "Dippy Duck." The series was hyped as the season's big hit. Unfortunately, TV audiences didn't agree, and *The Duck Factory* was canceled after only thirteen weeks. But it wasn't the right kind of show for Jim anyway. "They never used me, my way of getting laughs," he said. "They had thirteen episodes written before I was even cast."

After *The Duck Factory* flopped, Jim went back to performing at comedy clubs. In 1985, Rodney Dangerfield invited him to be his opening act in Las Vegas. The act featured a newer, zanier Jim Carrey. He'd go on stage with spiked hair and big red pants and make up funny bits on the spur of the moment. Sometimes it worked; sometimes it didn't. "Many, many nights I got no reaction at all," Jim said.

What was Rodney's reaction? "They were lookin' at you like you was from another planet, kid," he told Jim, shaking his head.

When Jim got back to planet Hollywood, he began to work even harder on his acting career. He won small parts in movies like the vampire comedy *Once Bitten,* starring Lauren Hutton, and the back-to-high-school flick *Peggy Sue Got Married,* starring Kathleen Turner. He played Johnny Squares, a self-destructive rock star, in the Clint Eastwood movie *The Dead Pool,* and Alien #2 in the sci-fi film *Earth Girls Are Easy,* starring Geena Davis. He scored a hit with his hilarious Showtime special, "Jim Carrey's Unnatural Act," and showed his dramatic talent in the made-for-TV movie *Doing Time on Maple Drive.*

But comedy was Jim's prime-time passion. In 1990, he got an even bigger chance to show millions of TV viewers just how frantically funny he could be.

The show was *In Living Color,* created and produced by African-American actor Keenen Ivory Wayans. Jim was introduced to Keenen by Damon Wayans, Keenen's brother. Damon had played Alien #3 in *Earth Girls Are Easy*. Keenan thought Jim's comic-from-Uranus style would be perfect for his fast-paced, irreverent comedy-variety show. He was right.

Jim came up with some pretty crazy characters on *In Living Color,* including grotesque-looking Fire Marshal Bill and pumped-up female body builder Vera de Milo.

"*In Living Color* was absolutely the best

place for me to be at that point, because they let me do pretty much what I wanted to do," Jim said. But he hated the crazy speed of television: "There was never time to do another take." (Doing another take means shooting a scene over again to get it right.) *In Living Color* won an Emmy award in 1990 for Outstanding Comedy Series.

Jim's work on TV netted him a whole new crop of fans. He had become known as a guy who could dream up totally off-the-wall characters and make them seem real.

So what was next for everyone's favorite Gumby-limbed gagmeister?

He took on the movie project that made him a real-deal, red-hot movie star!

On the set of *The Duck Factory* in 1984.

Jim and cast stir up some hot moves on the dance floor in the movie *Once Bitten*.

Filming *Earth Girls Are Easy* with Geena Davis, Jeff Goldblum, and Damon Wayans. Can you guess which one is Jim?

The cast of
In Living Color.

Ace baffles the police while searching for the Miami Dolphins' quarterback, Dan Marino.

Offbeat pet detective Ace Ventura gets help from his animal friends.

The always outrageous Ace finds the
kidnapped football star!

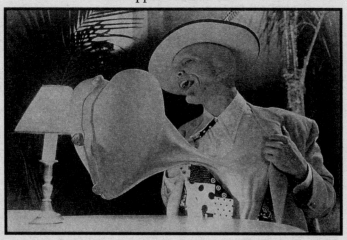

Jim, as The Mask, is overcome by love in
the smash-hit action-comedy.

Stanley Ipkiss rescues sexy lounge singer Tina Carlyle, played by Cameron Diaz.

The Mask singing "Cuban Pete."

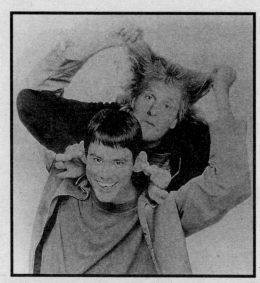

Jim and costar Jeff Daniels in the comedy *Dumb and Dumber*.

Dressed to kill at the Snow Owl Ball!

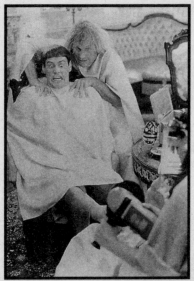

Harry Dunn (Daniels) looks on in horror as pal Lloyd Christmas (Carrey) gets a pedicure.

Lloyd Christmas, limo driver *and* ladies' man!

Jim and costar Cameron Diaz have fun at the Cannes Film Festival while promoting *The Mask*.

Jim and *Dumb and Dumber* costar Lauren Holly on their way to the premiere of *The Mask*.

Jim shares a laugh
with daughter Jane.

Jane helping Dad learn his lines.

Chapter 6

Cutting Loose as Ace Ventura

Ace Ventura: Pet Detective was famous even before it became a movie. It had gained fame in Hollywood as the project no actor would touch with a ten-foot boa constrictor!

That was before Jim Carrey got his hands on the script—and his head into the character of Ace Ventura. "I saw the script after everybody in town had already turned it down," he said. "And I didn't like it at all. I *did* like the idea of a pet detective, which was different." But he thought that the script was too corny as written.

The producers were desperate to get the film made, so they let Jim totally rewrite the screenplay. Smart move!

Jim turned *Ace Ventura* into a loony, gag-a-minute slapstick riot. The film was just right for introducing audiences to his special kind of frantic physical humor. Still often compared to Jerry Lewis, and comic Robin Williams as well, here Jim perfected his own style of comedy and created a unique rubber-limbed lunacy never seen before! The craziness starts in scene one and never lets up. It left audiences of all ages laughing themselves nearly out of their seats!

First, we see Ace working undercover as a delivery guy, carrying a package marked "fragile." Well, he's not exactly *carrying* it—he's playing soccer with it, doing rebounds with it, turning cartwheels over it as it smashes to the ground.

By the time the package gets to the customer, it's nothing more than a mass of broken glass. Ace goofs on the grungy, tough-looking customer, who's getting madder by the minute. A cute little dog appears in the doorway. Ace bends down to pet it. Then he exits stage left—fast. Once he's outside, we see the little pooch peek out from under his shirt. The scene shifts back to the mean-looking customer. He looks down and sees a toy dog instead of the real one. Ace has switched the dogs!

Ace Ventura, Miami's top (and only) pet detective, has done it again—he's rescued yet another purloined pet from the clutches of evil!

Back home, Ace tries to convince his seedy landlord he doesn't have any pets. But when he steps into his apartment, he gives a whistle. Seconds later, all kinds of animals come out of hiding to greet him. It's a magical moment in the movie.

Soon Ace comes face-to-face with the biggest challenge of his sleuthing career. Snowflake, the Miami Dolphins' mascot—a field-goal-kicking pet dolphin—has been kidnapped, and Ace is hired to find the animal. No one has much confidence in this goofy-looking gumshoe in a Hawaiian shirt, striped pants, boots, and shades, with his high-waxed hair parted on the side and spreading wide.

The plot thickens when Dan Marino, the Dolphins' star quarterback, is kidnapped, too. With a Super Bowl victory on the line for the "Fish," Ace is determined to find out whodunit and save the day.

Along the way there are nonstop laughs.

Jim, as Ace, imitates the crew members of

the Star Trek movie *The Voyage Home*, who went on a mission to save a whale. To cover up Snowflake's disappearance and get reporters away from the empty tank, he pretends to be Snowflake's German trainer. Jim moves in and out of all these characters faster than the speed of light. Later in the movie, Ace thinks he's got a suspect. It's Ray Finkle, a former Dolphins' placekicker. Finkle once missed a crucial field goal that cost the Dolphins the Super Bowl. He's vowed to get revenge on the team for blaming him for the loss.

Ace needs to investigate Finkle. That means getting inside the mental hospital where the placekicker once spent some time. Wearing a ballerina's pink tutu over rolled-up pants, Ace pretends to be a mentally messed-up football player so that he can get himself admitted to the hospital. While there, he shows how crazy he is by doing an instant replay in slo-mo—*backward*. He even does the announcer's voice backward in slow motion!

Then there's the famous scene in which Ace transforms the seat of his pants into a mouth so that he's talking through his backside. That was definitely a first for the movies—and quite a memorable moment!

Jim knew that he was taking a huge chance with *Ace Ventura*. So did *Ace* director, Tom Shadyac, a former stand-up comic himself who co-wrote the script with Jim. They worried that they had made *Ace* too way-out. "Every night we'd go, 'Oh, man, this is either gonna be big or the end of us both,'" said Jim. But he just went for it. "I figured it would either be a popular movie or it would ruin me. Completely." But Jim had fun making *Ace Ventura*.

Actress Courteney Cox, who played Ace's girlfriend, Melissa Robinson, in the movie, had fun, too. She loved working with Jim. "He's hysterical and so talented," she said. "That was one of my most fun movies ever."

When *Ace Ventura: Pet Detective* was released, movie critics ripped it apart. They called it "never funny" and "completely tasteless." But audiences loved Ace, and were truly "Carrey'd" away by the movie! And in the summer of 1994, the video was the number-one best seller. *Ace's* amazing success took everyone by surprise.

Now Jim was swamped with scripts from movie studios and production companies. Instead of being offered scripts other famous actors had turned down, Jim was now getting first crack. Everyone wanted to work with him. After fifteen years of struggling to make it, Jim Carrey had finally *aced* his way to the top!

Chapter 7

'Tooning into The Mask

Jim's next movie project, *The Mask,* gave him the chance to be something he'd always dreamed of becoming—a human cartoon! The movie features Jim's ability to stretch his face and body into amazing shapes, with a little help from special-effects studio Industrial Light & Magic. (ILM is the thirteen-time Oscar-winning studio that created all those incredible dinosaurs in *Jurassic Park.*) The combination added up to an unforgettable character and another hit movie for the king of slapstick comedy.

In the movie, a special mask changes shy Stanley Ipkiss from a bank-clerk dweeb in a suit into a mischievous but charming super-dude who turns Edge City totally topsy-turvy with his "Looney Tunes"–type antics.

Stanley, as the grinning, green-faced Mask, can spin like a tornado or morph into a cowboy or a weepy actress in a ball gown who's accepting an Oscar. He can dance at warp speed or freeze in midair. When he spots gorgeous singer Tina Carlyle at the CoCo Bongo Club, his eyeballs pop out like Slinkys, his jaw drops onto the table, and his heart shoots about a yard out of his chest. Tina Carlyle is played by model/actress Cameron Diaz, who makes her movie debut in *The Mask*.

Later in the movie, Stanley/The Mask and his faithful dog, Milo (who also gets to wear the Mask), are out to foil a team of bank robbers who are about to blow up the CoCo Bongo Club and everyone in it. The Mask can't let that happen, so he grabs the sticks of dynamite and swallows them. Suddenly, there's an earthshaking explosion, and The Mask's stomach swells to gigantic proportions. The pupils of his eyes spin around and smoke comes pouring out of his ears. Seconds later, The Mask calmly burps out a big orange fireball. "Wow," he said. "That's some spicy meatball!"

These are just a few of the visual effects ILM created for *The Mask*. How did they do it? With computers, of course. "We picked up where Carrey, the biological cartoon, left off," said Steve Williams, ILM's director of animation.

ILM used the same kind of groundbreaking high-tech computer animation they had created for the dinosaurs in *Jurassic Park*. But the animation whizzes at ILM had to admit that working on *The Mask* and watching Jim act like a live-action 'toon was more fun than making dinosaurs. "The craziest we could get in *Jurassic* was when we had the T. rex chomping on the lawyer," said visual effects producer Clint Goldman. "But 'crazy' on *The Mask* meant multiplying Jim Carrey's head by three and giving him four-foot bulging eyeballs. That was a lot more fun."

For one shot in the eyeball-bulging scene at the CoCo Bongo Club, ILM carefully measured camera height, lens width, and Jim's position in relation to the camera. Then they scanned the original sequence frame-by-frame into the computer. Next, they created three-dimensional drawings of outsize eyeballs. They put it all together and fine-tuned the effect by matching colors and shadings. In the last step, they added the film footage underneath the new image and printed the whole thing. This shot was one of ninety ILM turned out for this scene.

According to ILM, the most difficult special-effects challenges were creating computer-generated water for a whirlpool scene and turning Jim into "Flatman" when he jumps out of a window and is flattened on the pavement. But Jim was his own best special effect. "Jim is an amazing athlete," said *Mask* director Chuck Russell. "The guys from ILM told me that we saved a million dollars in optical effects because of the things Jim does for real. People wonder where *he* stops and the morphing begins."

The animation for *The Mask* was inspired

by the cartoon classics of Tex Avery, who helped create the famous "Looney Tunes" characters Bugs Bunny and Daffy Duck. In *The Mask*, Stanley Ipkiss watches Tex Avery cartoons after work, and his apartment features original cartoon art (called "animation cels") of Porky Pig and Daffy Duck. "I've always loved Tex Avery stuff," said Jim. "I went to ILM before we started shooting to see what they had in mind, and I found these guys sitting around watching cartoons. It was amazing." Jim felt he was exactly where he belonged!

Chuck Russell thought Jim and *The Mask* belonged together, too. "I'd seen his stand-up work and thought he was phenomenal," Russell said. When he started work on *The Mask*, he immediately went to Jim with the script. "Jim said, 'It looks like it's written for

48

me.' I said, 'You're absolutely right.'"

Russell and the movie's production company, New Line Cinema, didn't create the character of The Mask. It first appeared in a Dark Horse comic book of the '80s. The original Mask was a less evil version of the Joker in Batman comics. Chuck loved the character but wanted to make The Mask more lighthearted. He set the story in a more colorful world. He also saw The Mask as a very musical character. Jim himself got to sing in the movie, and his rendition of the disco-salsa tune "Cuban Pete" can be heard on the soundtrack album.

What were Jim's thoughts about *The Mask*? "One thing I think is really funny is a very weird guy who thinks he's totally cool," he said. "The Mask is a guy like that, and Ace was like that. But that's really the *only* way they're alike. In *Ace,* I'd show up in a Hawaiian shirt and sneakers and start filming. For *The Mask,* I had to be made up for four hours a day before we could begin to shoot."

The mask was created by Academy Award–winning makeup artist Greg Cannon. He fashioned a series of latex pieces that would let Jim's natural facial expressions come through. "Russell knew it would be pointless to bury my face under green gunk," said Jim. "The idea was to make the audience unsure of where my crazy facial expressions leave off and special effects begin."

Once Jim was made up and costumed as The Mask, a transformation took place. "I *became* The Mask," said Jim. "I could feel the character just burst through me."

Edge City, the slightly seedy metropolis

where *The Mask* takes place, wasn't constructed on a sound stage. Instead, the movie was shot entirely on location in Los Angeles. *Mask* production designer Craig Stearns used historic L.A. locations to give Edge City its own unique urban look. The Edge City Bank, where Stanley Ipkiss and his friend Charlie Schumacher work, was an old Bank of America building in downtown L.A. The designer combined the interior's old-fashioned marble floors, high gold-leafed ceilings, and arched doorways with modern furniture to give the set a timeless look. For the flashy CoCo Bongo Club, Stearns used the historic Park Plaza hotel, adding *Mask*-type touches such as palm trees and a running waterfall lit up by violet-colored spotlights.

It took Jim's comic genius together with a lot of behind-the-scenes talent to make *The*

Mask into a one-of-a-kind cartoon comedy. The hit movie has led to an upcoming animated TV show and a line of Mask toys. A sequel to *The Mask* is due out in summer 1996. What kind of mischief will the Mask make in *Mask 2*? Jim Carrey fans will just have to stay 'tooned!

Chapter 8

S-S-S-S-Smokin'!

Years ago, when Jim was struggling to make it as a comedian, he wrote out a check to himself for ten million dollars. The check said: "For acting services rendered by Thanksgiving, 1995." Jim showed the check to the audience during one of his many late-night talk-show appearances. Now that Jim is a *mega*movie star, it looks as if he may reach the ten-million-dollar goal sooner than he thought.

Ever since his success in *Ace Ventura*, Jim hasn't stopped making movies—and his salary just keeps growing with every movie he makes! Did he ever believe he would hit the jackpot so soon? "I don't know," he said. "I always believed in miracles. That's why I wrote that check to myself."

When Jim talks about his hard-won success, he said he's glad it happened the way it did: "Unless I had gone through all that disappointment, I don't think I would feel like I deserve it. As it is, I still, every once in a while, think, 'Ooh, what if they take it away?'"

No one can take away Jim's incredible talent. Audiences were treated to more Jim Carrey–style comedy in *Dumb and Dumber,* which opened in December 1994. "Guess which part I play?" Jim once said jokingly. In *Dumb and Dumber,* Jim plays Lloyd, a dimwit limo driver who falls in love with a beautiful client. He takes her to the airport but realizes she's left a briefcase full of cash behind. *Speed* co-star Jeff Daniels plays the nitwit driver of a dog-grooming van covered with fake fur. The two friends bumble their way on a cross-country jaunt in search of Lloyd's true love.

"Jeff Daniels is the sweet dumb guy," said Jim. "I'm the dumb guy who thinks he knows something." Jim's good friend Lauren Holly, of TV's *Picket Fences,* plays his dream girl in the movie. The two stars had fun playing practical jokes on the set.

In 1994, Jim also agreed to star in Ace 2, *Ace Ventura Goes to Africa,* a comedy called *The Best Man,* and, of course, *Batman Forever.*

Batman Forever is the third movie about the adventures of Gotham City's caped crusader. The first two starred Michael Keaton as Batman; the third will feature *Tombstone*'s Val Kilmer as Batman, alias millionaire Bruce Wayne. The character was first brought to life in a two-season TV series in the '60s. In the TV version, the villainous Riddler, Jim's role in *Batman Forever*, was first played by Frank Gorshin, a stand-up comic whose specialty was impressions. The second TV Riddler was John Astin, better known as Gomez Addams in the TV sitcom *The Addams Family*.

The Riddler, like the Penguin and the Joker, makes crime-fighting supertough for Batman. He drops silly riddles about crimes he's going to commit or has already committed. Then, when Batman solves the riddle and rushes to the crime scene, he finds himself in a trap set by the Riddler.

Jim came up with an idea about how he'd

like his Riddler to look: "You know how some people carve words and shapes into their hair? I want to carve a big question mark into the top of my head, and the period of the question mark would be made from the hair on the back of my neck." Cool. But he said there was just one hitch: "My hair may not grow back in time for me to do Ace Ventura 2."

Batman Forever director Joel Schumacher was thrilled to be able to add Jim's Riddler to the movie lineup of Batman baddies. He first saw Jim's act at an audition about ten years ago. "It was spellbinding," he said. "There was only one Jim, but it was like there were twenty people in the room, all of them different characters." Terrorizing Gotham City along with the Riddler in *Batman Forever* will be Harvey (Two-Face)

Dent, played by star Tommy Lee Jones.

Even though the hits and the movie-star perks seem to just keep coming, Jim isn't letting success trip him up. He's branching out into a new career as a songwriter, and he still takes his painting very seriously. Unfortunately, all his hard work and incredibly busy schedule took a toll on his marriage to Melissa. The couple is now divorced. "I don't have time for anything else right now but my work and my daughter. She's my first priority," Jim said. His daughter, Jane, sees her dad several times a week. "The only time it's tough is when I'm on the road or filming away from home, but fortunately that's not too often."

With his upcoming movies, his celebrity interviews, his painting, his songwriting, and his family, Jim still takes time to worry a little about the future. What's his worst nightmare? "I end up in a sitcom called 'Jim's Place,'" he said. "I'm from outer space—an intergalactic cop who crashes into the Chicago River and meets up with an earthling cop and solves crimes. That would be pretty bad." But what would be worse, according to Jim, is if he signed up to do Ace 5.

Right now, with all that hard-earned fame and fortune, Jim is sitting pretty, in his new home with a swimming pool, located in Brentwood, a wealthy L.A. suburb.

"I used to imagine myself with all this money and being sought after," he said. "It's not the money or the houses. That's really not it. What success means is being at the top of my game. That's what I want. What I'm still looking for." For the multitalented Jim Carrey, there's really no place to go but to the top.

"My parents taught me to believe in miracles," Jim said. "My life is proof that they exist."